Oversight Hearing on

Identifying Indian Affairs Priorities

for the Trump Administration

United States Committee on Indian Affairs

March 8, 2017

ISBN-10 1546931589

ISBN-13 978-1546931584

Table of Contents

Testimony
of
Ryan K. Zinke
Secretary
United States Department of the Interior
Before the
United States Senate
Committee on Indian Affairs
March 8, 2017

Good Afternoon, Chairman Hoeven, Vice-Chairman Udall, and Members of the Committee. Thank you for inviting me to testify before you today. I would also like to extend a thank you to my fellow Montana Senators, Steve Daines and Jon Tester, for their service on this Committee and for welcoming me here today. This is my first hearing since being confirmed as Secretary of the Interior and it is truly an honor to be here before the Senate Committee on Indian Affairs to discuss the Trump Administration's vision for Indian Country. I am also fortunate to share the panel today with an esteemed group of Tribal leaders from across the country. I look forward to working together with each of you as equals to grow and strengthen Indian Country.

I entered the Department just a few days ago, but the importance of my mission to partner with American Indians and Alaska Natives is one I do not take lightly. It is an issue of incredible importance to me personally. Regardless of political party, our duty as Americans is to uphold our trust responsibilities and consult and collaborate on a government-to-government basis with Tribes from Maine to Alaska.

Growing up in Montana, I learned very quickly that our Tribes are not monolithic. There are seven federally recognized Tribes in Montana, along with the Little Shell Tribe of Chippewa Indians who are in the midst of the federal recognition process. Each of them are spread throughout the entire state, working on their diverse priorities to provide for their people. In whatever form their economic development takes, from online lending to energy development, all tribes are sovereign and we must respect their right to self-determination.

In my experience, one thing is clear: sovereignty should mean something. As Montana's lone Congressman, I made it my priority to remain accessible to each of our Tribal members, from the Crow Nation to the Blackfeet Nation, so we could collaborate on their priorities on a leader-to-leader basis. I viewed them as equals, not rivals. We shared and debated our priorities and ideas while seeking common ground. As a warrior, I respected their culture and traditions greatly and I agree with the core value, 'if you have to fight, fight for your people.'

I am incredibly proud of the work Congress did to advance Montana tribes' priorities, such as the Blackfeet Water Rights Settlement, which was signed into law as part of the Water Infrastructure Improvements for the Nation (WIIN) Act. The warriors of the Blackfeet Nation, led by

Chairman Harry Barnes, greatly sacrificed time and resources for this historic achievement. Congress also made tremendous headway on the Little Shell Federal Recognition bill, which passed out of the House Committee on Natural Resources for the first time in history. And lastly, Congress worked with the Crow Nation to support their energy development potential by extending the Indian Coal Production Tax Credit and demanding their rightful seat at the table with the federal government to actualize their treaty rights. I am grateful to have Chairman A.J. Not Afraid sitting next to me today to tell his story about their future goals and priorities for success and look forward to working together in my new capacity of Secretary of the Interior.

I now have the honor to lead the very Department that, unfortunately, has not always stood shoulder to shoulder with many of the Tribal communities for which it is tasked to fight. Many reservations continue to struggle with high unemployment rates and a lack of business opportunities. Indian schools, roads, and houses are literally falling apart. Despite all this, the Administration has an opportunity to foster a period of economic productivity through improved infrastructure and expanded access to an all-of-the-above energy development approach. I fully understand that not all nations have access to energy resources or choose to develop them and I respect their position. As I have mentioned earlier, sovereignty should mean something and the decision to develop resources is one that each tribe must make for itself.

The President has remained steadfast in his commitment to infrastructure and seeks to address the excessive maintenance backlog that directly impedes our nation's economic growth and potential. Safe roads and bridges support Tribal economic self-determination by incentivizing investment in tribal communities. My team at Interior is already working to identify these top priorities within Indian country. I look forward to working with each of you here today and the Tribal leadership across our nation to continue this important discussion.

While economic development and infrastructure investments will play an important role in revitalizing Native communities, the immediate issues facing the Bureau of Indian Education must be addressed to ensure long-term stability in Indian country. I read the Government Accountability Office (GAO) High Risk Report for 2017; the determinations were disheartening and devastating. Words cannot capture how terrible it is that children in schools overseen by Bureau of Indian Education are so poorly served. Each of them deserves a high-quality education that prepares them for the future. Having served as Chairman of the Senate Education Committee during my time in the Montana State Legislature, I have a keen interest in education in rural communities. It is unacceptable that some of our students are attending schools that lack the most basic necessities, like insulation and clean water. We must also craft clear standards, develop measures for assessment, hire qualified teachers and principals to provide much needed leadership, and hold people accountable for mistakes. I do not expect to resolve these issues quickly, but I am personally invested in making real changes that will last.

There are plenty of other issues I know we will grapple with during my tenure at Interior. I have plenty to learn, but with your assistance I remain optimistic that we can work together with Tribes to foster stronger and more resilient Native communities.

Conclusion

One of the great privileges of my life was participating in the memorial ceremony for Michael Bell, a fellow Navy SEAL from the Fort Peck Assiniboine and Sioux Tribe. In between deployments in 2006, he was tragically murdered. Mike was a warrior I had the privilege of instructing as he began his SEAL career. To meet his family and pay respect to the life and sacrifices he made was truly humbling. In an incredibly moving tribute that same day, I was adopted into the Assiniboine family as an honorary member, and given a name and song.

I carry the honor of my traditional name, Wowonga Intacha, *Seal Leader*, with me today. As Secretary of the Interior, I will hold true the sacred words of my song, 'as I walk this road in life, I will help people as I go.' That said, there is strength in numbers, which is why I will need each and every one of you to assist me. This includes being accountable for your actions as we warrior ahead and make tough decisions to strengthen Tribal communities. In the SEALs, we are frequently reminded that "The Only Easy Day was Yesterday." As we begin the hard work before us, we must recognize that failure is not an option. I am here to listen, to accomplish your goals, and to move Indian Country forward to the best of my ability.

Thank you for the opportunity to share my views with the Committee. I look forward to working with you all and Tribes across the country to better the Bureau of Indian Affairs, Bureau of Indian Education, and all programs at Interior that impact Indian Country.

Testimony of Crow Nation Chairman Alvin Not Afraid, Jr.

I. Introduction

Good morning. On behalf of the Crow Nation, I want to thank Chairman Hoeven, Vice-Chairman Udall, Senators Daines and Tester, and the other distinguished members of the Senate Committee on Indian Affairs for holding this Oversight Hearing on Identifying Indian Affairs Priorities for the Trump Administration. My name is Alvin Not Afraid, Jr., and I am the Chairman of the Crow Nation. After serving 4 years as Tribal Secretary, I was elected Chairman last year and took office in December, 2016. I appreciate this invitation to provide testimony on economic priorities from the Crow Nation's perspective.

For many years, coal has been the mainstay of the Crow Reservation economy. However, various Federal regulatory initiatives during the previous administration in Washington, D.C. have taken a serious toll on the Western coal industry, and especially on the production of Crow and other Indian coal. My administration is aggressively pursuing other economic development projects, including renewable energy, to diversify and reduce our dependence on coal revenues, but those will take time – probably many years – to make major contributions to our efforts to achieve economic self-sufficiency.

Today, my testimony will focus on changes in Federal policies that will bring some much-needed near-term relief for Crow coal, while we transition to new clean-coal technologies, renewables, and other types of Tribal business enterprises. First, I'd like to give you some background on the Crow Nation and our Reservation lands, and our coal resources and development priorities.

II. Brief Overview of Crow Reservation, Land Issues and Resources

A. Brief History of Land and Development Challenges

The Crow Nation is a sovereign government located in southeastern Montana. The Crow Nation has three formal treaties with the federal government, concluding with the Fort Laramie Treaty of May 7, 1868. The Crow Reservation originally encompassed most of Wyoming and southeastern Montana, totaling 38.5 million acres. Through a series of treaties, agreements and unilateral federal laws over a 70 year span, Crow territory was reduced by 94% to its current 2.2 million acre area.

In addition to substantial land loss, the remaining tribal land base within the exterior boundary of the Crow Reservation was carved up by the Allotment Acts. By 1935, there were 5,507 Crow allotments, consisting of 2,054,055 acres. The Big Horn and Pryor Mountains were not allotted and still remain reserved for the Crow Nation and its citizens.

The Crow land base has been further decimated by fractionated ownership of various allotments. The Department of the Interior ("DOI") estimated that over 10% of all fractionated lands within Indian country are actually within the Crow Reservation (with many parcels of allotted lands that have more than 100 owners).

During 2014 - 2015, the Crow Nation partnered with DOI and meaningfully addressed the fractionation issue through implementation of the *Cobell* Settlement. The Crow Land Buy-Back Program resulted in more than $130 million paid out to Crow landowners, with more than 240,000 equivalent acres purchased for the Crow Nation.

Despite the success of the Crow LBBP, the overall loss of the Crow land base and allotment have resulted in checkerboard ownership of reservation lands, giving rise to overlapping governmental authority (federal, state, tribal and local). Sometimes, the land issues become cost prohibitive for project developers. As discussed later, tax incentives and other measures are critical in order to level the playing field for Indian energy projects.

B.   *Present Land, Population, and Education*

Today, there are 14,000 enrolled citizens of the Crow Nation, with more than 9,000 of those residing within the exterior boundaries of the Reservation. Our Tribal membership consists of many young people – fully 58% of our members are under 30 years old. This demographic only reinforces the need to take a long-term view of the Reservation economy.

Our goal is to invite more of our citizens to return home to live and resume tribal relations, but we must be able to offer homes, jobs, and a place to find their dreams. Our current unemployment rate is between 25% and 47%, depending on whose statistics you use.

The Crow Nation has always emphasized higher education and we currently have more than 400 annual applications for higher education assistance. Because of federal funding limitations and internal budget constraints, however, we can only partially fund 90 students each year. In addition to providing financial support for education, we have a separately chartered tribal college (Little Bighorn College, "LBHC") that started operations in 1981. Among the hundreds of LBHC graduates, many are employed on and around the Crow Reservation in a variety of positions including teachers' aides, computer technicians, office managers and administrative assistants.

C.   *Crow Coal – Past, Present and Future*

1. The Absaloka Mine

The Crow Nation has very substantial undeveloped coal resources, estimated at 9 billion tons. The Crow Nation has developed a limited amount of its resource, by leasing a portion of its coal reserves for the past 40 years to Westmoreland Resources, Inc. ("WRI"). WRI owns and operates the Absaloka Mine ("Mine"), suppling Powder River Basin coal to Midwestern utilities, and it has produced 200 million tons of coal since 1974. From the Mine's 5-7 million tons per year of coal production, it provides production taxes and royalties to the Crow Nation – exceeding $20 million in 2010 when the Mine was operating at full capacity. **The revenue generated from the Mine has represented as much as two-thirds of the Crow Nation's non-federal budget.**

Furthermore, WRI employs a 70% tribal workforce, with an average annual salary of over $66,000, and is the largest private employer within the Crow Reservation. The importance of the Mine to the economy of the Crow Reservation cannot be overstated. Without question, it is a critical source of jobs, financial support and domestically-produced energy. WRI has been the Crow Nation's most significant private partner over the past 40 years. During 2012-2013, the Tribe and WRI finalized a new lease agreement to extend the life of the Absaloka Mine for two more decades.

However, as my Administration begins its efforts to bring prosperity to the Crow people, the future of the Absaloka Mine has never been more uncertain. Production at the Absaloka Mine has fallen to only 3 million tons per year, and will stay at that level for at least the next 2 years. This is despite the previous Tribal administration agreeing to a reduction in our coal severance tax rates, which further compounds the loss in Tribal revenues.

In the past, Tribal royalties and coal severance tax revenues from the Mine totaled well over $20 million per year, but it is now projected that we will receive **less than one-half those amounts for the next few years.** This large reduction in coal revenues has had a drastic effect on the Tribal Government workforce, including major layoffs and furloughs, and greatly reduced the levels of essential government and emergency services that we are able to provide for our membership.

2. The Big Metal Project

The Crow Nation has worked for many years to expand development of our vast coal resources. In 2013, the BIA approved our agreement with Cloud Peak Energy ("CPE") to explore, with options to lease and develop an estimated 1.4 billion tons of Crow coal in the southeastern corner of the Crow Reservation. This long-term project, named "Big Metal" from a Crow legend, will also provide much needed revenue to the Crow Nation, increase employment opportunities for Crow and Montana citizens, and diversify Tribal revenue sources.

Cloud Peak Energy (CPE) has demonstrated their commitment to both safety and the environment, and we appreciate their leadership as one of this country's largest coal producers. In addition, CPE has been a good partner with the Crow Nation, providing college scholarships to dozens of Crow students and supporting those in need. All of this has occurred while CPE has worked with the Tribe to complete exploratory drilling, secure surface rights, assess cultural resources that will need to be protected, and begin environmental base line work for the permitting process, all of which has been ongoing since 2014.

However, the Big Metal project faces the same challenges as the Absaloka Mine, with domestic coal markets steadily contracting due to Federal coal policies that have had a disproportionate impact on Tribal coal development. In addition, full development of the Big Metal project is largely dependent on coal exports to the Pacific Rim through ports in the Northwest, but efforts to expand coal export capacity through those ports have been consistently stymied by environmental challenges aimed at killing coal.

3. The Clean Coal Future

Finally, the Crow Nation has long recognized that the long-term benefits of our very large coal resource will depend on new clean coal technologies that address concerns with climate change. I would like to continue to build the first coal-to-liquids ("CTL") plant in North America with full carbon capture and utilization.

In 2008, the Crow Nation and our partner signed a project agreement to develop the Many Stars project, a coal-to-liquids project that would produce up to 50,000 barrels or more per day of ultra-clean jet and diesel fuel. The Crow Nation sought to contract with the U.S. Air Force and other local industries to supply clean fuel that would meaningfully reduce carbon emissions throughout the world, reduce America's dependence on foreign oil, and provide a safe and secure domestic fuel supply to our national defense.

Unfortunately, with the recession and financial crisis that hit in 2009, it became impossible to obtain the large investment needed for this type of cutting-edge project. Since then, there has been no concerted Federal policy to encourage the development of clean coal technology, carbon capture and sequestration, or other technologies and incentives that could save many good coal jobs throughout the country.

III.   Crow Nation Coal Policy Priorities

There are a number of changes in Federal policies and incentives that the Congress and the Trump Administration should take to provide both near- and long-term benefits for the continued, responsible development and production of Crow coal, while we diversify our Reservation economy to achieve economic self-sufficiency.

A.   The OSMRE Stream Protection Rule

First, I want to thank the Congress and President Trump for enacting the joint resolution under the Congressional Review Act disapproving the Office of Surface Mining's misguided Stream Protection Rule.

The proposed new regulations published by OSM in 2015 were originally intended to address some practices in the Eastern coal mines, but included onerous and unnecessary new requirements for Powder River Basin mines as well. The proposed new Rule was developed without input from the West, and based on my discussions, neither the Federal or State regulators would have been able to implement it.

The Rule was also developed without meaningful consultation with the Crow Tribe, as required by Federal law, on the 2,000 pages of materials that accompanied the proposed rule. Unlike mines regulated by State authorities under SMCRA, the Rule would have had an immediate effect on the Absaloka mine which OSM regulates directly on Crow Reservation. It would have reduced the Mine's coal reserves, and further reduced sales of Crow coal at a time when the Tribe is already suffering from diminished coal production and prices.

We are greatly encouraged by this early and timely action to prevent devastating impacts on the mining of Crow coal. As further explained below, the mining of Crow coal is already subject to one of the most extensive regulatory programs in any industry under the Surface Mining Control and Reclamation Act (SMCRA), which the Crow Tribe has been working to assume authority to administer on our own lands.

B. EPA's Clean Power Plan

EPA's "Carbon Pollution Emission Guidelines for Existing Stationary Sources: Electric Utility Generating Units," otherwise known as the "Clean Power Plan," was initially proposed in 2014 and required States to reduce carbon dioxide emissions from existing coal-fired power plants. Although it would have a major impact on the markets for Crow coal, it was developed without any consultation with the Crow Tribe, as required by Executive Order 13175. The Crow Nation and the Montana Attorney General sent joint comments to the EPA in December 2014, to express grave concern about the negative impact on the Crow Nation. Nevertheless, EPA finalized the proposed rule in 2015 without further Tribal consultation or consideration of these impacts.

The Clean Power Plan has already had a serious negative effect on Crow coal and the Crow Reservation economy. The great majority of Crow coal from the Absaloka Mine has been supplied to the Sherburne County Generating Station ("Sherco") near Minneapolis. However, as a result of Minnesota's efforts to comply with the Clean Power Plan, Units 1 and 2 at Sherco will be shut down soon. For Unit 3, which was designed for Crow coal, and is the largest, most modern and cleanest unit, the longer term future remains uncertain.

The Clean Power Plan must be rolled back to prevent further adverse impacts on Crow coal customers, especially on the newest and cleanest generating units that still have many years of productive life.

C. Indian Coal Production Tax Credit – Leveling the Playing Field

In addition to the EPA's Clean Power Plan, numerous practical problems consistently arise with each proposed Indian coal project. The lease approval and development process is burdensome, slow, and complicated. Federal regulatory requirements for appraisals, surface access approvals and environmental assessments to conduct exploration within the Reservation often create significant delays. Further, incomplete land records, inadequate BIA staffing, and surface land fractionation (described above) create uncertainty that discourages investment and significantly impedes project development. It is extremely difficult to compete with off-reservation development because of these problems, even with the best efforts of particular BIA employees and the Crow Nation.

The Indian coal production tax credit ("ICPTC"), originally enacted in the 2005 Energy Policy Act, has kept the Absaloka Mine open and competitive since 2006. This $2+ per ton tax credit is intended to "level the playing field" for Indian coal (currently Crow, Navajo and Hopi), by offsetting some of the additional regulatory hurdles we face. This credit neutralized the threat of a potential mine closure and continued the Absaloka Mine's ability to provide critical employment and revenue for essential Crow governmental functions. Under our agreements with Westmoreland, it has also yielded several millions of dollars in direct benefits to the Crow Nation, funds that are sorely needed now.

However, since 2013, the ICPTC has been extended on a year-to-year basis as part of the tax extender packages, and that has diminished its effectiveness by not providing certainty to support major long-term investments necessary for coal development. Worse still, it expired at the end of 2016.

In order to overcome all of the additional regulatory burdens and land transaction issues described above, the Crow Nation seeks a permanent extension of ICPTC. With this tax incentive made permanent, the Crow Nation would have the opportunity to compete with others on a level playing field. It will help sustain the Absaloka Mine, produce additional Tribal revenue, and encourage new coal development like CPE's Big Metal project.

As mentioned above, the development of new coal utilization technologies will be very important to ensure the long-term economic viability of the Crow Nation's large coal resources. In addition to permanently extending the ICPTC, the Congress and the Trump Administration should focus on providing other tax incentives and direct support for clean coal technologies and carbon capture and sequestration. These measures will allow us to resurrect the Many Stars coal-to-liquids project in a modified form to produce ultra-clean fuels while addressing the criticisms of climate change advocates.

D.   *Access to International Markets*

With the contraction of coal demand for utilities in the United States, the best hope for maintaining and expanding Crow coal production is the export market, primarily to modern new coal plants in Japan and South Korea. For example, major development of Cloud Peak Energy's Big Metal project on the Crow Reservation depends primarily on being able to export our coal, and an expanded marine export facility on the West Coal is essential infrastructure to support that effort. It also is important to note that Powder River Basin coal from Crow mines is lower in sulfur dioxide and nitrogen oxide, which is better for the environment than the coal that is currently mined in Asian countries.

The Army Corps of Engineers recently denied permits for the Gateway Pacific Terminal, which would have provided the closest and most efficient way to ship Crow coal overseas. Also, protests to expanded rail shipments of coal from mines to the ports have been used to impede the environmental permitting process for new coal ports.

The last proposed new coal export terminal is the Millennium Bulk Terminals project in Longview, Washington. The Crow Tribe trusts that the Congress and the new Administration will ensure that the Army Corps and other Federal agencies do not unnecessarily delay or deny the needed permitting for this important project and others that may be developed in the future.

E. Tribal Primacy Under SMCRA

The Surface Mining Control and Reclamation Act of 1977 (SMCRA), created the U.S. Department of Interior's Office of Surface Mining and Reclamation Enforcement (OSMRE), and a comprehensive nationwide regulatory program for surface coal mining. The Act authorizes States to assume primary enforcement responsibility with OSMRE's approval and oversight, which has been done in most coal states including Montana.

The 2006 amendments to SMCRA authorized Tribes to also assume primary responsibility for its administration on Reservation lands. The Crow Tribe has been working diligently with OSM for several years to complete the requirements for undertaking this complex regulatory program. In 2009, the Crow Legislature enacted the Crow Coal Mining and Reclamation Act, which has undergone an extensive, detailed informal review by OSM. Trained Tribal personnel of the Crow Coal Regulatory Office (CCRO) currently participate in all inspections of the Absaloka Mine. In the future, we foresee undertaking full responsibility for new coal mine permitting with the time and funding to build capacity for this highly technical function.

As a sovereign nation, the Crow Tribe has the right to regulate our own lands and resources. What remains of the Crow Reservation will be our Nation's homeland for all time, and we have a continuing vital interest in protecting our people, land, air, water, wildlife and cultural resources from any negative effects of mining our valuable coal resources.

We trust that Secretary Zinke and the Congress will continue to support the Crow Nation's efforts to assume SMCRA Primacy, with the necessary funding, OSM staffing, and flexibility to accomplish this important task. For our part, I am taking measures to re-invigorate and prioritize the Tribe's work to satisfy the requirements for assuming Primacy, and look forward to working with OSMRE and the other DOI agencies toward a timely completion.

For the Crow Nation at this pivotal time, the importance of SMCRA Primacy extends beyond just coal mining. We also have substantial resources of Gravel, Limestone, and Bentonite that are economically viable, and will help diversify the Reservation economy.

SMCRA Primacy is a stepping stone toward the extension of Tribal sovereignty to regulating development activities for these other minerals as well. When we have developed and demonstrated our capability to regulate surface coal mining under the most stringent requirements of SMCRA and Tribal law, the Tribe will most certainly be in a position to assume responsibility from the Bureau of Indian Affairs (BIA) and the Bureau of Land Management (BLM) for protecting the Reservation environment during development of these other Tribal mineral resources.

We also look forward to working with the Committee and the Secretary to adopt legislation and policies as necessary to facilitate the Crow Nation's regulation of other mineral development on our Reservation homeland.

F.   Abandoned Mine Lands Reclamation Fund

For many years, the Absaloka coal mine paid a 35 cent-per-ton Reclamation Fee to the Federal government for the Abandoned Mine Lands fund. That Fee, currently 28 cents-per-ton, amounts to a Federal tax on Crow-owned coal, reducing the amounts of royalties and taxes that the Crow Nation could otherwise collect.

One of the other changes made by the 2006 SMCRA amendments was to authorize the return of a portion of the AML fund to the certified States and Tribes who have completed reclamation of most of their old abandoned mines. For the Crow Nation, this has meant several millions of dollars in funding, not only for old mine reclamation efforts but also for new infrastructure and community development projects.

However, there have recently been recurring efforts to divert certified States' and Tribes' shares of the AML fund to pay for Eastern coal miners' retirement benefits. While we understand concerns with the cutbacks in other funding, it is not fair or appropriate for Crow coal to subsidize those benefits, especially when we have so many immediate and pressing needs ourselves.

The Crow Nation hopes that the Congress and the new Administration will support the continued return of the AML funds to the certified Tribes and States from whom the Reclamation Fee is collected.

IV.   Conclusion

Given our vast mineral resources, the Crow Nation can, and should, be economically self-sufficient. My administration, like others before it, desires to develop our mineral resources in an economically sound, environmentally responsible manner that is consistent with Crow culture and beliefs. More than anything, we desire to improve the Crow people's quality of life, create a future with good-paying jobs and employment benefits within the Crow Reservation, and provide hope and prosperity for the next seven generations of Crow citizens.

By leveling the playing field for developing clean Crow coal for domestic markets, exports and coal conversion, we firmly believe we can help ourselves while simultaneously meeting national energy goals -- achieving energy independence, securing a domestic supply of valuable energy, and reducing the country's dependence on foreign oil.

Mr. Chairman and Committee members, thank you again for the opportunity to testify on these important subjects before you today. I would be happy to answer any questions.

STATEMENT OF
THE HONORABLE KEITH B. ANDERSON
VICE CHAIRMAN
SHAKOPEE MDEWAKANTON SIOUX COMMUNITY

Oversight Hearing on
Identifying Indian Affairs Priorities
for the Trump Administration

SENATE COMMITTEE ON INDIAN AFFAIRS
March 8, 2017
2:15 p.m.
628 Dirksen Senate Office Building

INTRODUCTION.

Good afternoon, Chairman Hoeven, Senator Franken, Members of the Committee, Secretary Zinke, fellow tribal leaders.

On behalf of my Shakopee tribal government, I want to thank the Committee for this opportunity to describe our great expectations for –
- What Secretary Zinke will be able to accomplish at the Interior Department, and
- What we hope are priorities for the Trump Administration.

LET ME BEGIN BY SHARING A BIT OF BACKGROUND ON THE SHAKOPEE TRIBE.

For centuries, my Mdewakanton ancestors have lived in the larger area surrounding what remains today of our Shakopee Reservation. We Dakota people have stood our ground, even as the great cities of Minneapolis and St. Paul have grown up around us, bringing both opportunities, and challenges, to our tribal community.

The Shakopee Tribe has played a key role in the economic revitalization of our region. Our tribally-owned and controlled enterprises are a vital source of governmental revenue for ourselves and for many of our neighbors.

For years, the Shakopee Tribe has been the largest employer in Scott County, and regularly is awarded the honor of being one of the "top work places" in Minnesota.

The Shakopee tribal government has forged over 60 inter-governmental agreements with our neighbors, for whom our Tribe provides essential governmental services in such diverse areas as –

- top-flight fire and rescue;
- state-of-the-art waste water treatment;
- alternative wind and solar energy production;
- large-scale organics recycling;
- diverse transportation planning and development; and
- mobile medical and emergency command centers.

The Shakopee Tribe is the largest tribal donor in Indian Country, annually giving 18 million dollars or more in grants to less fortunate Indian tribes and community organizations. In recent years, we have focused our efforts on the production and distribution of food and information that supports healthy lifestyles, contributing over 5 million dollars to efforts to strengthen Native food sovereignty.

"SOVEREIGNTY" IS WHY THE SHAKOPEE TRIBE BELIEVES SECRETARY ZINKE IS WORTHY OF SUPPORT.

From his days in the House of Representatives to the day he was nominated Secretary, Mr. Zinke has shown that tribal sovereignty is at the top of his list of priorities.

As Interior Secretary, Mr. Zinke will fill a key role in the government-to-government relationship with Shakopee and every other tribal government. As lead trustee, Secretary Zinke has a solemn responsibility to honor and protect our sovereignty, self-governance, and self-determination.

All of what the Shakopee Tribe does, for others, and with other governments, rests on one basic foundation – the Shakopee Tribe is a <u>government</u>, a <u>sovereign</u>, worthy of respect by other sovereign governments.

Shakopee is a text book example of the fact that, when tribal governmental sovereignty is respected, economic success follows.

At the same time, any attack on our core tribal identity - any bypassing of our sovereignty as inconvenient - is a direct assault on our culture and way of life.

By definition, tribal sovereignty is expressed and exercised in different ways. Respecting sovereignty means the rest of us honor the decisions each tribe makes for its own people, its own resources, its own territory. Sovereignty is a tribe's shield against the arrogant hegemony of outsiders who think they know what's best for a tribe, whether they are called local governments, conservationists, environmentalists, federal trustees, or hungry corporations.

Secretary Zinke understands and respects tribal sovereignty. The Shakopee Tribe looks forward to working with him and his colleagues in the Trump Administration to preserve and protect tribal sovereignty in ways that advance tribal self-determination and self-sufficiency.

HERE ARE SOME PRIORITIES THAT SECRETARY ZINKE CAN HELP PRESIDENT TRUMP ADDRESS.

President Trump took office a few weeks ago promising change for the regions of America that the federal government has long ignored. By any measure, that includes much of Indian Country.

The Shakopee Tribe will ask Secretary Zinke to ensure that the Trump Administration's infrastructure initiative is shaped to enable Indian Country to catch up to the rest of America. That will mean allocating public funds to extend new infrastructure into rural America so that Native American communities can finally have an equal opportunity to access jobs, markets, education, health and other services on par with the rest of Americans without having to move away from our homelands. It will also mean that Secretary Zinke, as the lead federal trustee for tribes, will have to work hard with every federal agency to ensure they adhere to meaningful consultation with each tribal government affected by a proposed federal action. Meaningful consultation means real, open, early, and responsive mutual decisionmaking in partnership with tribal governments.

We will ask Secretary Zinke, as Indian Country's leading advocate within the Trump Administration, to forcefully support meaningful tax reform that allows only tribal governments – no other governments – to tax economic activity on Indian land. This would end the heavy burden of dual taxation in Indian Country. And it would spur private sector investment in what would be low or no-tax tribal empowerment zones. This kind of bold, big idea would restore the territorial sovereignty of tribal governments over their economies. We will also ask Secretary Zinke to encourage more targeted and robust tax credits for investment in Indian Country.

We will ask Secretary Zinke, as the steward of America's trust responsibility toward Indian tribes and Native Americans, to protect and expand federal financial support for essential governmental services in Indian Country that have been systematically and chronically underfunded for generations. We will encourage Secretary Zinke to make maximum use of direct funding to tribal governments through the Indian Self-Determination and Tribal Self-Governance authorities, and thereby curb the federal bureaucracy's tendency to consume limited federal funding before it can reach Indian Country. When Secretary Zinke and President Trump face competing pressures to allocate scarce federal funds, we will ask Secretary Zinke to remind his colleagues in the Administration of the many contributions in blood and treasure that Indian Country has already made to the welfare of the United States. The Shakopee Tribe's financial success in the gaming market is an exception to the experience of most tribal governments, and so we will ask Secretary Zinke to help preserve the federal funding that is owed all Indian tribes under the trust responsibility._

And finally, we will ask Secretary Zinke to take the lead within the Trump Administration to secure early enactment of the Tribal Labor Sovereignty Act of 2017, Senator Moran's bill -- S. 63. That bill would restore seven decades of legal precedent by treating tribal government employers the same as all other sovereign governmental employers. This bill is not about labor unions, it is about tribal sovereignty, about our tribal right to set our own laws for our own employees on our own lands.

Mr. Chairman, thank you for this opportunity to outline some new directions we believe are worthy of support from Secretary Zinke and President Trump. I would be most pleased to answer any questions you may have.

TESTIMONY OF

CHICKASAW NATION LIEUTENANT GOVERNOR JEFFERSON KEEL

BEFORE THE

U.S. SENATE COMMITTEE ON INDIAN AFFAIRS

MARCH 8, 2017

Chairman Hoeven, Ranking Member Udall and members of the committee, thank you for inviting me to testify in today's important hearing to identify Indian Country priorities for the new Trump Administration. My name is Jefferson Keel. I serve as the Lieutenant Governor of the Chickasaw Nation and speak today on behalf of Chickasaw Nation Governor Bill Anoatubby and the people of the Chickasaw Nation.

We look forward to working with and supporting Secretary Zinke in protecting our treaty rights and carrying out the federal trust relationship to tribes. Full federal recognition of tribal sovereignty, as that status is recognized in the United States Constitution, is of paramount importance to Indian country. We look to this Congress and the Trump Administration to continue the long-standing federal policy of engaging with tribal sovereigns on a government-to-government basis. This principal is fundamental to all issues that will come before you arising from Indian country.

Federal policies supporting American Indian tribal self-determination and self-governance grows directly from the government's respect for the importance and value of tribal sovereignty. It is a simple fact that these policies work because they rest on the core principal that tribal peoples are in the best position to address the issues affecting their own communities. This committee has helped lead the way in crafting policies that support tribal self-determination and self-governance, and while we have accomplished great things, much remains to be done.

All too often, federal statutes and regulations treat tribal governments differently than every other form of government. While the Constitution establishes tribal governments as sovereigns with rights and responsibilities similar to those of states, in practice, policies are almost always more restrictive for tribes. Indian country has, accordingly, long called for parity—for the treatment of tribal sovereigns in a manner consistent with what states and other sovereigns within the United States system are afforded by federal law. Indeed, given the federal fiduciary obligation to protect tribal sovereignty, we believe our argument for such treatment is even stronger than the states, in many instances.

We commend the new administration's policy to affirm and commit to existing tribal consultation policies, which establish frameworks for meaningful government-to-government engagement and collaboration. We believe such frameworks are essential to a high functioning federal-tribal dynamic and call on this Congress and Administration to deepen and enhance its commitment to effective consultation, wherever and whenever possible. We believe *all* executive departments and agencies should consult and collaborate with tribes on the development of federal policies with tribal implications, and we believe this is true whether the government is considering the establishment of a new statutory or regulatory provision or the repeal or abrogation of an existing one. Doing so will strengthen our government-to-government relationship and further empower the unparalleled progress made in Indian country since the advent of these policies in the late-1960s.

One example of this body's pragmatic responsiveness to strengthening the federal law's provision of parity to tribal sovereigns is recent action relating to the National Labor Relations Board. Several years ago, the Board administratively set aside decades of settled policy and law and determined, notwithstanding its own profession of having no expertise in federal Indian law, that tribal actors are not all entitled to the protection of tribal sovereignty. Specifically, the Board concluded that non-tribal labor organizations could assert the protections of the National Labor Relations Act against tribal government employers—treating tribal governments in a manner that no state or territory has ever been subjected to. The Chickasaw Nation litigated the matter for several years before the Board finally acknowledged that our sovereignty and treaties with the United States demand the parity of treatment we claimed. But other tribes do not benefit from our treaties, and nothing necessarily precludes the Board from again changing its mind as to what respect it should afford these sources of federal law. I want to thank this committee and our champion on this issue, Sen. Jerry Moran, for recognizing the untenable position in which this put tribal sovereigns and the quick approval of S.63, the Tribal Labor Sovereignty Act. Mr. Chairman, I respectfully urge you to work closely with your colleagues to bring this important issue to a vote by the full Senate as soon as possible. Basic fairness and adherence to long-standing policies regarding tribal sovereignty would support such action.

We also urge swift action to reauthorize the Native American Housing Assistance and Self Determination Act (NAHASDA) by the committee and the Senate. For several years running, the House has overwhelmingly passed a NAHASDA reauthorization with a large bipartisan majority, but Indian country has been forced to wait on reauthorization in the Senate because one or two senators have put holds on the measure—blocking the will of the body and ignoring the needs of Native peoples. This issue is too important to let another two years go by without approval. Indian country and this successful program deserve better.

Another timely issue of critical concern is the status of the Indian Health Care Improvement Act. That measure was permanently reauthorized after a decade-long bipartisan effort to enact the measure; however, it was unfortunately tucked into the Affordable Care Act in 2010. The Indian Health Care Improvement Act, which stands apart from the rest of the Obamacare measures, is critical to the provision of health care throughout Indian country and must be safeguarded in any effort to change federal health care laws.

There are a number of other issues inside the Affordable Care Act that I would like to bring to the committee's attention. We believe, for example, that the employer mandate represents an unwarranted intrusion on tribal self-government. In addition to health services to our tribal citizens, the Chickasaw Nation provides generous health care insurance coverages to all its employees—benefits that far exceed the standards in the prevailing market—and the Act's mandate created complications and burdens where no problem could be shown. We would also point out that the Act uses a definition of Native Americans that differs from that found in other parts of the U.S. Code and the regulations, which has been widely acknowledged as a drafting error over the years. We urge the committee to correct this error in any legislation on the subject. Finally, tribal health departments have well developed third party payer arrangements with Medicare, Medicaid, the Department of Veterans Affairs, and other federal programs. Congress should pay careful attention to nuance and detail in overhauling the Act so that these relationships are not inadvertently disrupted or unsettled.

We applaud the President's commitment to the veterans who have served and proudly serve today to protect our great nation. On a daily basis active duty members become veterans, and too many veterans return home to find that their greatest challenges still lie ahead. The Chickasaw Nation is committed to finding the path for our veterans to become leaders, both in the community and tribal government, teachers, business owners, active citizens and successful parents. We work closely with the US department of Veterans Affairs and have established a good relationship with the Office of Tribal Government Relations in the VA.

President Trump has spoken for many months about a wide-ranging infrastructure package. We support the concept of vigorously investing in our nation's roads, airports, waterways, water and sanitation systems, and other critical infrastructure. Indian country has, for generations, faced chronic shortages of public and private investment in this area, which adversely affects public safety as well as opportunities for sustainable economic development and self-sufficiency. We believe tribes should be full participants in any and every program authorized by Congress for the rehabilitation of aging or the development of new infrastructure. We further believe funds for such projects should flow directly to tribes rather than be run through state governments, which have not always adequately addressed Indian country needs. In Oklahoma, we work closely with our colleagues in local government and the Oklahoma Department of Transportation to identify and execute projects that help the entire community but are of particular importance to tribal citizens. Without an ability to bring funds under our control to the bargaining table, tribal needs and interests would likely not receive the prioritization they deserve.

We believe tax reform would present great opportunities to incentivize tribal investment and bring badly needed opportunities to Indian country. We commend the Native American Financial Officers Association and the outstanding work they have done identifying workable tax and pension reforms that would have an immediate beneficial impact on tribal economies. In particular, we commend efforts to repeal the "essential governmental function" rule that applies to tribal bonds and which forces tribes to maintain two separate pension or employee retirement programs. Members of this committee and the Senate Finance Committee have been working hard to address this particular matter, and we thank you. Your success in these efforts would have tremendous positive impact on Indian country.

We also believe that the New Markets Tax Credit program has already demonstrated its utility for Indian country development and suggest the program should be expanded and stabilized. The Chickasaw Nation was recently awarded a $20 million allocation and is facilitating economic development projects throughout Indian country with these monies—

projects that are creating jobs, enhancing infrastructure, and deepening service provision and tribal entrepreneurship. We previously used a New Markets Tax Credit allocation to completely redevelop an outdated and dilapidated Indian Health Service facility in Ada, Oklahoma, to serve now as the Carl Albert Service Center, a multi-purpose tribal government facility. Both the construction and the operation of this new facility has been an economic and programmatic boon to the community. We believe Congress should support the allocation of a stable revenue stream to support the implementation of this program in Indian country.

The Chickasaw Nation works closely with the federal government in the provision of a wide variety of services to our citizens. Often times, we administer federal programs under 638 self-governance compacts. We have been a leader in the Indian Health Service's joint venture program—which we used in conjunction with $220 million of our own funds, to construct and equip three health facilities, including the 80-bed Chickasaw Nation Medical Center in Ada, Oklahoma, which serves American Indians throughout southeast Oklahoma. Our facilities in Ada, Ardmore, and Tishomingo provide critically needed health services in this region, which we operate in conjunction with other services and programs addressing suicide prevention, mental health and substance abuse, child welfare, domestic violence, and sexual assault. Without continued federal support for self-governance compacts, Indian country, American Indians, our citizens would be deprived of these programs and services, and we commend you for your continued commitment to ensuring that the compacting system remains strong and vital to the federal-tribal relationship.

We appreciate Congress's passage of the Violence Against Women Act, which statute is key to the protection and well-being of American Indian women—among the most basic responsibilities of any government. This legislation provides American Indian tribes the tools to enable to do even more to help keep Native American women safe through effective law enforcement and prosecution. We thank you for your continued support for this measure, now and when it is due for reauthorization.

Our own work under the Violence Against Women Act supplements our other law enforcement programs throughout the Chickasaw Nation. We have made it a priority to work closely with federal, state and local law enforcement agencies within a complicated jurisdictional landscape to protect and serve all citizens of Oklahoma, and federal support for these efforts through the Self-Governance Compact and Community Policing Act is important to continued success of the Chickasaw Lighthorse Police.

Additional governmental services include the Johnson-O'Malley education program, high school equivalence tutoring and testing. Education has long been a high priority for the Chickasaw Nation. Therefore, we request the Chickasaw Nation High School Equivalency (HSE) testing centers and certification and transcript issuing processes be certified and recognized by the U.S. Department of Education. While the U.S. Department of Post-Secondary Education currently only recognizes state-issued HSE transcripts, the Chickasaw Nation HSE testing center policies are set up to adhere to equivalent security and testing practices as those of state recognized testing centers. We have a signed and approved Educational Testing Service contract in place to provide the HiSET exam which is one of three HSE tests federally recognized by the U.S. Department of Education and has been approved in 21 states. The exam aligns itself to the College and Career Readiness Standards for Adult Education.

Broadband internet availability is an important aspect of the infrastructure challenges facing Indian Country. Tribal citizens access only internet connectivity speeds that are far below the FCC broadband standard. This limitation stifles economic development, technical advances like tele-medicine, and negatively impacts education by accelerating the already increasing homework gap. Current federal funding models are aimed primarily at for-profit businesses and often focus on specific institutions that provide too little service to those in need. Tribes are dedicated to improving the lives of the traditionally underserved including tribal citizens, rural schools and health care institutions, and those living in economically depressed areas. Directing funds to groups such as tribes could improve the likelihood of these funds benefiting those who need it most, and we ask that you remember Indian country when considering any measure to upgrade the country's internet availability.

Chickasaw identity is founded upon a unique and special heritage embodied in our language, our sacred sites and our traditional knowledge. Repatriation of our ancestors' remains is extremely important to us. The repatriation process, however, can take many years to complete. The Chickasaw Nation aboriginal homeland in the southeastern United States is rich with generations of our ancestors, including archaeological sites and sacred burial places. In 2016 the Chickasaw Nation actively pursued 21 repatriations, which will allow us to take care of 4,034 of our ancestors and thousands of their funerary objects. We ask the government to continue to provide supportive funding for tribal repatriation efforts, both culturally affiliated and culturally unidentifiable. We further ask that you consider developing legislation to aid indigenous peoples seeking the international return of ancestors and items of cultural patrimony.

Finally, I want to touch on a recent announcement by the Department of the Interior about reforming the Indian Trader Act and attendant regulations. We believe this effort to be representative of the well-intended work by career staff across Administrations of both parties. We support this effort and believe there is good work to be done on this front. We would, and will, encourage the Department both to modernize the regulatory framework and to streamline mechanisms for tribes to conduct direct oversight of the federal regulatory system via appropriate self-governance compacts. We would, and will, also urge the Department to proceed carefully in its effort—with the principal of "do no harm" clear and foremost in mind. Given the complexities of the federal common law of Indian affairs, any statutory and regulatory change must be approached carefully and with due consideration of potential unintended consequences. Indeed, a number of important Supreme Court decisions rest on the preemptive scope of the Indian Trader Statutes and implementing regulations. In attempting any update of those laws, the Department must not displace or alter the careful balance of sovereign interests that those decisions uphold. While we support update and reform—indeed, we would applaud it—we also ask that caution be observed in all future actions.

Thank you for your time and for holding this important hearing. I look forward to answering your questions.

Written Testimony of Paul Torres
Chairman of the All Pueblo Council of Governors

"Identifying Indian Affairs Priorities for the Trump Administration"

Senate Committee on Indian Affairs
Oversight Hearing
March 8, 2017

Thank you Chairman Hoeven, Vice Chairman Udall, and members of the Committee for this opportunity to provide testimony on Identifying Indian Affairs priorities for the Trump Administration. The All Pueblo Council of Governors in New Mexico thank you for your dedicated work as champions of Indian Country in the United States Senate.

My name is Paul Torres and I am the Chairman of the All Pueblo Council of Governors (APCG), which is comprised of tribal leaders (Governors) from the 19 New Mexico Pueblos and the Pueblo of Ysleta Del Sur in El Paso, Texas. I also serve as the Governor of the Isleta Pueblo. The APCG is the oldest Native American group of tribal leaders, constituted and formed in 1598. Collectively, the leadership of the APCG is respectful of the historic relationship between the Pueblos and the U.S. Government. In the spirit of cooperation, based on respect and full consideration of the sovereign status of tribes, the leadership of the Pueblos wishes to establish a meaningful relationship with the new Administration. In order to maintain trust and good will, the All Pueblo Council of Governors offer these statements of concern and policy considerations for the benefit of the Trump Administration.

Introduction. The history of the Pueblos has its beginnings over 10,000 years ago. Many still occupy their traditional homelands, with their original governmental structures sound, their languages, ceremonies, and their belief systems still intact. They have a long and varied history dealing with foreign governments such as Spain and Mexico. Unlike other tribes in the United States, Pueblo land status is unique and falls under the 1848 Treaty of Guadalupe Hidalgo, 9 Stat. 922 (1948). The leadership of the All Pueblo Council of Governors stands committed to strengthening their relationship with the United States Government. We look forward to working with the new Administration to collectively tailor an approach that recognizes and acknowledges tribal sovereignty, assures a continuous government to government relationship, allows tribal economies to achieve their full economic potential, is respectful of traditional belief systems and draws on the intellectual capacity, talent and contributions of Pueblo People to the growth and development of this great country.

1. Government-to-Government Consultation

The U.S. Constitution acknowledges that Indian Nations, Tribes, and Pueblos are separate distinct governments within our federalist system. The historic roots of the government-to-government relationship between the Pueblos and the United States Federal Government are symbolically embodied in the "Lincoln Canes." President Lincoln gifted the canes to the Pueblos in 1863 as a formal acknowledgement of their inherent right to self-governance. Passed down through the generations, the canes serve as revered symbols of tribal sovereignty, governing power, and authority over tribal land, natural resources, and residents.

Establishing a strong federal government-to-government relationship with all tribes was formalized in modern times by a number of Republican Presidents including President Nixon, who supported and signed off on major Native American legislation, and President Ronald Reagan through his Native American policy positions. Presidents George W. Bush and his father George H.W. Bush affirmed government-to-government consultation requirements.

Of critical importance are long-standing Executive Orders requiring regular and meaningful consultation between the Administration and all federally recognized tribes on matters that have tribal implications. The Executive Orders on consultation seek to ensure respect for and the strengthening of the tribal-federal relationship, and to reduce the imposition of unfunded federal mandates upon Indian tribes. These orders require federal agencies to meaningfully consult with Indian tribes prior to formulating policies that could affect tribal governments or tribal communities. These Executive Orders have provided the Pueblos opportunities for dialogue with federal agencies on issues that directly affect tribal communities and are pertinent to the federal government's trust responsibility - a legal and moral obligation by the federal government to tribes. While not perfect, the consultation process is key to forging a strong government-to-government relationship. We urge the Trump Administration to reaffirm and strengthen the practice of meaningful tribal consultation and communication long carried out by prior administrations and Presidents intent on recognizing and respecting the American Indian and Alaska Native people of America.

2. Federal Trust Responsibility – an Obligation to Indian Tribes

The United States Constitution, treaties, federal statutes, executive orders, Supreme Court precedent, and other agreements set forth the federal government's recognition of Indian tribes as sovereign nations with inherent powers of self-governance over their communities and tribal members. They also establish the federal government's trust responsibility to protect the interests of Indian tribes and communities. The federal workforce and annual budgeting process help fulfill these unique obligations to Indian tribes by carrying out the federal government's commitment to work with tribes on a government-to-government basis by ensuring the effective administration and funding of Indian Country programs.

Federal Indian Budget. The Trump Administration recently released its budget blueprint for Fiscal Year 2018 in which the President proposes to cut approximately $54 billion in discretionary non-defense spending. These across-the-board cuts are alarming because the majority of programs serving Indian Country fall under the category of discretionary spending and are not exempted under the President's proposed plan. These programs exist across the federal government in agencies such as the Bureau of Indian Affairs, Indian Health Service, Department of Agriculture, Forest Service, and the Environmental Protection Agency, among many others. Budget cuts to these programs pose an immediate and unacceptable risk to the health, safety, and welfare of our people, lands, and natural resources. When combined with the fact that Indian tribes are more reliant on federal funds than most other communities, it becomes clear that any comprehensive cuts to the federal budget without specific carve-outs for Indian Country programs will necessarily have a disproportionate impact on tribes. We, therefore, urge the Trump Administration to exempt Indian Country programs from any proposed budget cuts to fulfill the federal government's trust obligations to Indian tribes.

Providing sufficient federal funding to meet the critical needs in Indian Country is a chronic and well-documented challenge. The Pueblos support a budgeting process that allocates federal funds based on need, rather than a specific formula. Such an approach would be responsive to the range of needs and internal capacities of federal agencies administering Indian programs. Needs-based federal funding also would provide agencies such as the Indian Health Service, Bureau of Indian Affairs, and the Bureau of Indian Education with the resources necessary to begin to recover from years of underfunding and program cuts.

Federal Hiring Freeze and Proposed Workforce Reduction. Endemic vacancies in the workforce pose a constant challenge to federal programs serving the complex needs of Indian Country. The Indian Health Service, in particular, struggles to recruit and retain qualified medical and administrative staff at its facilities, despite the continual increases in the number of Native patients using their services. The federal hiring freeze and proposed federal workforce reduction threaten to severely diminish the already strained ability of these programs to provide high quality services to our people—services that the federal government is obligated to provide as part of its treaty and trust responsibilities to Indian tribes. The Pueblos, therefore, urge the Trump Administration to adopt measures that ensure the federal hiring freeze and proposed federal workforce reduction will not apply to programs serving Indian tribes.

3. Infrastructure - a Requirement for Economic Advancement

Deficiencies in Infrastructure Limit Development and Housing Opportunities. Many Pueblos are economically distressed rural communities. Infrastructure development is key to developing, diversifying, and sustaining tribal and rural economies. However, most tribal lands have conditions that require intense overhauling - roads are often unimproved, utilities are insufficient, and internet and broadband barely exists. In addition, other types of infrastructure critical to creating vibrant tribal communities, including residential construction, are deficient or lacking. The result is a severe housing shortage on tribal lands.

Limited Access to Capital Restricts Economic Development. Tribal business transactions have become increasingly sophisticated and often involve non-native partners, investors, and lenders. However, limited access to capital and financing remains one of the most significant barriers to Pueblo economic development. Tribes across the country spend an incredible amount of time and resources defining, developing, and defending programs, but programs alone do not transform economies and communities the way economic investment does. It is important to create investment funds, resources, and models that are mutually advantageous to tribes and investors for economic advancement, stability and diversification. The opportunity for a decent income, a desirable job, a comfortable living and a chance to provide for family is a desire of all Americans.

Build-Out of Digital Infrastructure Can Bridge the Urban-Rural Divide. In this modern technological age, a great digital divide exists and needs to be filled in order for tribal governments to function, for schools to provide sound educational opportunities, and for tribal communities to maintain consistent communication beyond tribal boundaries by acquiring technological information, data and research. Digital infrastructure allows remote access to high school, secondary and post-secondary education on-line courses, as well as medical care technology, which may otherwise be difficult, if not impossible, to access in many rural communities. Better access to digital infrastructure such as broadband, Internet services, and digital platforms, is also essential for business development, which will be key for economic participation and competition by the Pueblos.

The Pueblos are Major Contributors to the Southwest Economy. Pueblo governments and Pueblo owned business enterprises are collectively among the largest employers in the state, providing thousands of jobs in many rural areas of New Mexico. Most recent job figures put the number of jobs provided by tribal governments and enterprises at nearly 18,000 statewide in various industries. Non-Indians hold nearly 75% of these jobs. Some of the Pueblos have become regional economic engines. In the case of most tribal enterprises, these jobs stay in the community. Many tribal members also spend their money off reservation, pay federal taxes, and in many instances pay other taxes such as property and state income taxes. Pueblo members engaged in off-reservation commerce also pay gross receipts and other taxes. All this contributes to tribal, state and local economies. The Pueblos struggle with uniquely burdensome federal restrictions and regulations, poor infrastructure and other challenges that limit their economies from flourishing. Pueblo leadership, therefore, places a high priority on economic development and diversification and the creation of well-paying sustainable jobs for our people.

Tax Policy. Pueblos are functioning governments with a unique place in the federal legal system. This causes complications, not the least of which occur in the tax arena. Any legislation addressing tax reform should address these issues by clarifying how tribal governments will be treated, thereby eliminating the disparate treatment of tribal governments and reducing confusion.

What the Pueblos Support

In order to continue and enhance their contribution to the tribal, state and national economic landscape, the Pueblos support infrastructure and tax reform such as: funding for on-reservation infrastructure projects that promote sustainable job creation initiatives and that attract investment to Indian Country; strengthened housing for Pueblo communities provided under the Native American Housing and Self Determination Act of 1996; the provision of direct access to federal Low Income Housing Tax Credits; clarification of the treatment of Indian tribes and Pueblos as other governments for purposes of federal tax provisions such as tax-exempt bonds, pensions, charities, the child adoption tax credit and other provisions; and tax and infrastructure policies that encourage investment on tribal lands.

4. Ensure Affordable, Accessible Quality Healthcare

Native Americans have some of the worst health statistics in the country. The Indian Health Service (IHS) is the primary source of healthcare for Native Americans. However, the IHS has never been fully funded, and as a result, services are rationed, limited, inconsistent, unreliable and sometimes taken at "your own risk." In addition, many tribes now pursue P.L. 93-638 contracting and/or compacting of services from IHS. This trend is an indicator that tribes believe healthcare can be better provided by other delivery mechanisms in addition to IHS. To promote and provide reliable and quality health system and services, it will be important for this Administration to develop policies that significantly improve the IHS budget and also allow for other forms of healthcare delivery to tribal communities.

Preserve the Indian Health Care Improvement Act. The Indian Health Care Improvement Act (IHCIA) provides the basic program, structure, management, and budget formulation for the Indian Health Service (IHS). The IHCIA was permanently enacted by cross reference in Section 10221 of the Affordable Care Act (ACA). Although the ACA was the legislative vehicle through which the IHCIA reauthorization was passed, the IHCIA predates and is independent from the ACA. Woven throughout the ACA are other provisions that directly pertain to Indian health, including Medicare Part B billing (Section 2902), tax exclusions for Indian health benefits (Section 9021), and payer of last resort provisions for Indian health programs (Section 2901). The IHCIA also allows IHS and tribal health programs to collect Medicare and Medicaid reimbursements for services provided to Native patients at non-IHS facilities. Because the IHS has been historically underfunded at only 43% of need, these third-party payments are a critical source of supplementary financial assistance for the delivery of Indian healthcare services. The Pueblos urge the Trump Administration to preserve the IHCIA and protect Indian-specific provisions of the ACA in the course of any effort to repeal or amend the ACA.

Maintain Medicaid Expansion to Protect Indian Health Benefits. Pueblo leaders are concerned that a number of the ACA-related proposals would sunset Medicaid expansion, which has provided desperately needed funding to supplement woefully underfunded Indian healthcare providers, including IHS and tribally-run facilities. Due to funding limitations, many IHS facilities have had to reduce direct access to specialty care providers, intensive care, inpatient care, and emergency room services. Medicaid expansion and Marketplace coverage allow Native patients to access these services at private or non-IHS facilities at reduced cost. The Pueblos urge Congress to maintain increased patient access to critical services through Medicaid expansion.

Additional congressional proposals would cap Medicaid funding by moving to a block grant or per capita allocation formula rather than a Federal Medical Assistance Percentage (FMAP) formula, which could transfer or shift Medicaid funding responsibilities from the federal government to state Medicaid programs. Under FMAP, the federal government covers 100% of Medicaid costs for Medicaid-eligible services "received through" an IHS or tribal healthcare facility, including through the Purchased/Referred Care (PRC) system. The 100% FMAP program alleviates state costs associated with the provision of Medicaid services, helps tribes with service delivery and data collection management, and improves patient access to critical care.

The increase in reimbursements through Medicaid expansion has strengthened the internal capacity of our Pueblos to meet the healthcare needs of communities. For example, Santo Domingo Pueblo has expanded access to diabetes care, dental health programs, and behavioral health services, while also adding over thirty employees to the local workforce. Taos Pueblo also recently opened a residential substance abuse and mental health treatment center focused on the needs of Native youth, and the Pueblo of Jemez Comprehensive Health Center was designated as a full-service Federally Qualified Health Center (FQHC) capable of receiving special Medicare and Medicaid reimbursement. The Pueblos urge Congress to maintain Medicaid expansion in those states that have chosen to participate to protect Indian health benefits and advance the delivery of desperately needed services in Indian Country.

Exempt the IHS from Federal Budget Sequestration. Access to and the delivery of quality healthcare in Indian Country is further complicated by annual cuts to the IHS budget due to sequestration. All other critical healthcare agencies, such as Veterans Affairs, were exempt from the full effect of funding reductions during the federal budget sequestration of 2013— except for the IHS. The disruption in federal funding has resulted in a loss of over $219 million and counting from the IHS budget. This translates into immediate and long-lasting negative health impacts through lost resources for primary and preventative healthcare services, staff recruitment and training, and other programs serving our communities. The Pueblos recommend that the IHS be given parity with other healthcare agencies through an exemption from sequestration, as well as any freezes of the federal budget.

What the Pueblos Support

The Pueblos understand that the new Administration has made it a priority to repeal and replace the ACA to revise its terms and improve affordability. However, they caution that repealing or amending the ACA might do unintentional but catastrophic harm to Indian healthcare delivery and access. To this end, the Pueblos respectfully request the Administration to exempt the Indian Health Care Improvement Act Reauthorization of 2010 from repeal efforts, preserve Indian-specific provisions of the ACA, consider Indian health care programs and services as mandatory spending programs, and exempt them from the potential return of sequestration to the federal budget, and to consider funding increases to Indian health programs and services and policy initiatives that provide alternatives for quality health care.

5. Land Base, Water and Natural Resources - Important Tribal Assets

Continuation of the Land-into-Trust Program. As sovereign tribal nations, the Pueblos exercise an inherent right to self-governance that is strengthened by our ancestral connections with the land. The ability of the federal government to take land into trust on behalf of tribes is, therefore, essential to our self-determination. Trust lands enable us to provide a homeland for our people as well as a base from which to offer essential governmental services, such as, housing, education, healthcare, and economic development opportunities. Trust lands also facilitate the expression of our identity as Pueblo people by protecting the natural and cultural resources that form the bedrock of our traditional practices. We urge the new Administration to continue to support the land-into-trust program as a means of strengthening tribal governments, economies, and communities across our great country.

Wise Stewardship of Natural Resources. The stewardship of land, minerals, water and other natural resources is key to both the economic well-being of Pueblo people and to their cultural survival. Every day the Pueblos strive to balance these interests.

The vast majority of federal lands are carved out of the ancestral homelands of Indian tribes. The historical and spiritual connection of tribes to federal lands was never extinguished. Courts acknowledge that Indian tribes retain rights to hunt, fish, and gather on federal lands. Federal laws acknowledge the continued right of tribes to access federal lands to pray, conduct ceremonies, and gather medicinal plants. Federal laws and executive orders also require federal land managers to consult with tribal governments prior to taking action that would affect the integrity of federal lands. For example, the Pueblo of Laguna is working with the Department of Agriculture and the Forest Service as a Cooperating Agency in the preparation of an Environmental Impact Statement for the Cibola National Forest Plan Revision. Such beneficial partnerships better ensure that tribal interests are taken into consideration in the development of the federal land resource and management plans.

The Pueblos ask the Trump Administration to partner with them in strengthening these rights and access to ancestral homelands and sacred places located on federal lands. If the Administration considers transferring lands out of federal control, we respectfully ask that the Pueblos be provided the right of first refusal to ancestral homelands and sacred places. Pueblos and other tribes are proven stewards and managers of their lands and forests. Protection of and access to natural resources is important not only to the Pueblos but to all Americans.

Affirming Tribal Water Rights and Water Quality. The Pueblos have been engaged in major court battles to secure tribal water rights as provided under federal law. The federal government must remain committed to supporting tribal water claims. Pueblo water rights are not mere claims on paper, but reflect a long term, historic Pueblo presence, cultural identity and willingness and desire to live on their traditional, ancestral lands. The settlement of these rights also provides stability and economic benefits to surrounding communities. For these reasons, water, land and air must remain protected from contamination that results from mining and extraction activity including uranium mining, oil and gas production and transportation. All such activity that would affect tribal interests should be advanced only with tribal consultation and consent.

Preservation of Bears Ears National Monument. In keeping with our traditional role as stewards of the land, the All Pueblo Council of Governors has worked closely with federal, state, and local governments to protect important landscapes and cultural sites in the southwest, including the area now known as the Bears Ears National Monument in Utah. Our ancestral ties to the Bears Ears cultural landscape extend to time immemorial and can be traced through the ancient roads, dwellings, petroglyphs, and ceremonial features that continue to enrich the region today. However, these sites are under constant threat by erosion, vandalism, looting, and indiscriminate damage through off-road vehicle use, as well as the general degradation of wildlife and plant habitats that are significant to our traditional practices. We urge the Trump Administration to preserve the designation of Bears Ears as a National Monument to support the permanent, long-term protection of the land and its invaluable cultural and natural resources.

Protecting Tribal Cultural Patrimony. Disturbing and unsettling occurrences at national and international auction houses as well as in the art world have led to outrage and condemnation by many tribes throughout the United States, including the Pueblos. These occurrences include the illegal trafficking in and the selling of Native American cultural property - items considered sacred, sacrosanct, used in worship, and should never to be given away or sold. These items are not works of art; they are integral parts of a Pueblo's living cultural identity and spiritual practices.

We remain grateful to the leadership of the Senate Indian Affairs Committee for your support of the PROTECT Patrimony Resolution, H. Con. Res. 122 (Dec. 2016). The Resolution puts in place greater deterrents to prevent the theft and illegal trafficking of our sacred items, both domestically and abroad, and promotes the protection of our identities as Pueblo People by better ensuring that items of cultural patrimony remain within our communities. However, a significant amount of work remains to be done on this important issue. We look forward to working with you and the Trump Administration on strengthening the implementation of the Native American Graves Protection and Repatriation Act (NAGPRA), and advancing the Safeguard Tribal Objectives of Patrimony Act (STOP Act) during the 115th Congress.

What the Pueblos Support

In the Pueblo worldview, we are stewards of the earth's natural resources - land, water, air, and minerals. The Pueblos support policy and legislation that provide protection of natural resources, includes funding to support management of these resources, and policy that requires Federal-Tribal collaboration when natural resources and cultural properties are affected in any way. The Pueblos support a policy that requires in-depth collaborative efforts to arrive at mutual outcomes where natural resources on or near tribal lands could be destroyed or diminished. In addition, the Pueblos seek support for pending federal legislation that would clarify existing laws and condemn the trafficking of sacred items. The Pueblo leadership asks the new Administration to support Congressional proposals to protect cultural patrimony.

6. <u>Pueblo Destiny Lies in the Control of Education</u>

High Standards Are Critical. Pueblo leaders wish to create a highly skilled, well-educated, workforce within their respective tribal communities. With a pool of qualified workers, the Pueblos believe they will be able to attract business and economic development possibilities, create well paying job opportunities, and assure that tribal members enjoy a prosperous future that comes with being well educated.

Education System. The Pueblos of New Mexico have always supported sound educational programs that comply with state and federal accountability standards. We emphasize the importance of high quality instruction, effective professional teacher development and the development of appropriate, culturally sensitive curriculum, including Native language retention and instruction. In addition, Pueblo leaders support comprehensive oversight of the flow of funds and the implementation of policies that effectuate meaningful educational change. It is important to foster the advancement of higher education, but also to consider re-introducing vocational education, which in many school districts has been eliminated or severely limited. Vocational education can provide skills that contribute to employment opportunities and sustainable incomes. In addition, Science, Technology, Engineering and Mathematics (S.T.E.M.) curriculums must be incorporated into tribal school systems.

Protecting and Preserving Native Languages. The Pueblo worldview is contained in their languages. In addition to maintaining tribal life ways, the Pueblos have established various programs and methods in order to retain and preserve what are considered some of the most ancient and distinct languages in America. Some Pueblo languages are so unique they are not spoken anywhere else in the world. Students in language immersion programs demonstrate substantial improvement in their academic performance and testing. Data shows that Native students excel in S.T.E.M related subjects largely attributable to their language skill set. Native languages offer a unique thought process and a way to interpret the world and its interactions.

What the Pueblos Support

The Pueblo leadership supports policies that provide educational opportunities and resources in order to begin cultivating the next generation of Native students who are able to achieve academic success, perform proficiently on standardized tests, and graduate. A number of Pueblos are taking over the operation of Bureau of Indian Education (BIE) schools located on tribal lands. Operating and maintaining schools requires considerable resources. It is important that the new Administration provide adequate funding to support tribal schools and initiatives like S.T.E.M. The Pueblo leaders also urge the new Administration to realize the value of Native languages and support funding for programs that prevent the further loss of language, traditions, and culture.

7. <u>Appointment of Native Americans to Key Trump Administration Positions</u>

Pueblo governments and their communities can be severely affected in many different ways by the actions of the U.S. government through policy or the enactment of federal law. Therefore, it is extremely important that the voice of the 20 Pueblos be heard and considered, especially with regard to appointments to key positions within the Administration that will affect the Tribes, Pueblos and Indian Nations in this country. Equally important is the appointment of Native Americans to key positions within all federal agencies across the Administration. The 20 Pueblos respectfully ask that the President seriously consider Native American professionals for appointment to the following key positions:

- Special Advisor to the President on Native American Affairs, The White House
- Deputy Director for Tribal Affairs in the White House Office of Intergovernmental Affairs and Public Engagement
- Deputy Secretary, Department of the Interior (DOI)
- Assistant Secretary for Indian Affairs, DOI
- Director, Bureau of Indian Education, DOI

- Solicitor, Office of the Solicitor, DOI
- Director, Indian Health Service, HHS
- Director, Administration for Native Americans, HHS

We also respectfully request that the Trump Administration maintain "Office of Tribal Relations" / "Native American Programs" (OTR) officials in each department / agency of the government to help facilitate access by tribal government leaders to the federal programs designed to benefit tribal, state and local governments. Agencies that have OTRs include, among others, USDA, Justice, Commerce, Veterans Affairs, the EPA, Treasury, Health and Human Services, Energy, Labor and Homeland Security. As with the above listed positions, many qualified Native Americans currently serve or could serve in these positions.

Finally, because federal laws and the development of federal jurisprudence have a disproportionate impact on the daily lives of Indian Country residents, we ask that the Administration make it a priority to strongly consider appointing Native Americans to serve as judges in the federal court system.

Conclusion

Federally recognized tribal governments are and have for centuries been acknowledged as distinct political and sovereign entities recognized in the U.S. Constitution, treaties, federal laws and regulations, and federal court decisions. Prior to contact with other nations, Indian tribes exercised powers of self-government over their territory, residents, and visitors. Their sovereignty pre-dates the Constitution and is derived from the fact that they owned all the land that is now the United States, including the state of New Mexico. The U.S. Constitution acknowledges the sovereign status of Indian tribes in the Treaty Clause, in the 14th Amendment as "Indians not taxed," and in the Commerce Clause. Separate sovereign tribal groups are a vital part of the fabric of this great nation. Working together, with a common understanding of history, with mutual respect and recognition of the obligations of the relationship forged by President Lincoln, as symbolized by the Lincoln Canes, and with an optimistic view of the future, the Pueblos look forward to successfully working with the Trump administration.

www.ingramcontent.com/pod-product-compliance
Lightning Source LLC
Chambersburg PA
CBHW081134280526

45787CB00007B/3073